loving

for life

for life

loving

for life

loving

for life

loving

loving

for life

Presented to:

From:

This is my prayer: that your *love* may abound
more and more in knowledge and depth of insight.
Philippians 1:9

Requests for information should be addressed to:
    Inspirio, the Gift Group of Zondervan
    Grand Rapids, Michigan 49530

Compiler: Sarah M. Hupp
Assistant Editor: Molly Detweiler
Design: Big Cat Marketing Communications

Printed in China
00 01 02 03 /HK/ 5 4 3 2 1

# loving
# for life

secrets to a lasting relationship

inspirio
The gift group of Zondervan

Cherish Each Other

ost of us have no greater desire and prayer than a lifetime of love and commitment to one person with whom we can share life. Marriage is one of God's greatest gifts to humanity. It is the mystery of living as one flesh with another human being (Ephesians 5:31–32).

Marriage is first and foremost about love. It is bound together by the care, need, companionship, and values of two people, which can overcome hurt, immaturity, and selfishness to form something better than what each person alone can produce. Love is at the heart of marriage, as it is at the heart of God himself (1 John 4:16).

*Dr. Henry Cloud &
Dr. John Townsend*

*T*he dictionary defines *love affair* as "an affinity between two persons … a particular experience of being in love." The particular experience we are concerned with is the wonderful life-long love affair God designed for husband and wife. As the Creator of marriage and the author of love, his provision includes a love affair full of thrills and joy and lasting satisfaction for *every* couple.

It is God's will in every marriage that the couple love each other with an absorbing spiritual, emotional, and physical attraction that continues to grow throughout their lifetime together. You and your partner can have a wonderful love affair. And you can cause it to happen.

*Dr. Ed Wheat*

*U*nderstanding the components of love—trust, mutuality, honesty, intimacy, pleasure, and sex—will help you create your own diamond-studded love life. Far from being a marital add-on, a healthy, creative love life is a key to a healthy marriage.

*David and Claudia Arp*

*C*hoose to love each other. It's not a feeling. It's not even passion. Love is a choice that we make. It's an action that we choose to take toward that person we love. You aren't in love; you *do* love.

*Robert and Rosemary Barnes*

*A man will leave his father and mother and be united to his wife,*
*and the two will become one flesh.*
Ephesians 5:31

*Above all, love each other deeply, because love*
*covers over a multitude of sins.*
1 Peter 4:8

*I found the one my heart loves.*
*I held him and would not let him go.*
Song of Songs 3:4

*May you rejoice in the wife of your youth.*
Proverbs 5:18

*God is love. Whoever lives in love lives in God,*
*and God in him.*
1 John 4:16

*How beautiful you are*
*and how pleasing, O love,*
*with your delights!*
Song of Songs 7:6

*O*ur heavenly Father, who gave us bodies as well as souls and spirits, meant for the body to be nurtured through the beauty of marital love. If there is anyone who ought to have a romantic life, it is the couple whose relationship is based on the will and the Word of God!

We should joyfully participate in the intimacy God has provided in and through our spouse. Such romance and intimacy involves care, conversation, respect and physical satisfaction in the arms of your beloved. All of our interplay and intimacy helps to build a strong marriage. When you discover this beautiful romance in a marriage relationship, you will enjoy a rare gift indeed!

*Charles R. Swindoll*

$\mathcal{D}$uring the courtship days, you probably had limited exposure to your fiancé. It was easy for each of you to put the other's needs or best interests first since you didn't have to do it twenty-four hours a day. Obviously, if your fiancé was putting your best interests first and fulfilling your needs to the neglect of his own, your heart was melting daily in response to him, and vice versa.

After marriage, things quickly changed. The exposure was no longer limited to times when you were both "at your best." For each, your own interests began to take precedence over the other's.

Typically, most of us expect our mates to retain their original physical and emotional attractiveness. But a funny thing happens on the way to retirement … we change. And if we change the things our mates once found attractive, we have to replace them with something better. What specifically can you do to increase your inward beauty that is naturally reflected through your eyes and facial expressions and definitely increases your attractiveness?

*Gary Smalley*

We keep hoping that our marriage partner will perceive our emotional needs, perhaps by extrasensory perception, and unselfishly set out to meet them. The inner child, always in residence within us, waits expectantly for the perfect fulfillment of all our dreams.

The only possible approach to this innate egocentricity of ours is to apply literally the formula of Jesus: "Give, and it will be given to you" (Luke 6:38). Instead of demanding, or expecting, that another will fulfill our needs, we must become mature enough to ask, "How can I discover and satisfy the needs of my partner."

*Cecil G. Osborne*

13

# Treasure Each Other

Touch each other—Give hugs and kisses often!

Spend time together—Eat a snack together
alone and enjoy the quiet time.

Encourage each other—Leave loving messages
on sticky notes, lunch bags, answering machines, etc.

Keep romance alive—See a romantic movie;
always kiss good-bye; keep a picture of the two
of you in plain sight.

Share your thoughts and feelings—Write a letter telling
your spouse why you'd marry him or her all over again.
Unconditionally accept each other.

*W*e hold a great portion of each other's self-esteem in our hands. A husband who loves his wife will counteract the critical world his wife lives in. Let her know she's beautiful. Let her know she is loved for who she is as a person. She doesn't need to hear from her husband about her flaws. She's painfully aware of them already.

*Robert and Rosemary Barnes*

"*C*herishing" means holding dear, nurturing, and celebrating. Cherishing your marriage includes verbalizing your love and commitment to your spouse and demonstrating that love in little, meaningful ways throughout your lifetime—and in big, spectacular ways every now and then. It means encouraging each other and affirming your relationship in private and in public. And it means celebrating your love for each other.

*David and Claudia Arp*

The husband is supposed to work on seeing the need for a close relationship that his wife has. Then he's to step out of what he's comfortable doing and meet that need. It's his sacrifice.

The wife is to submit to the needs of her husband. She's to be his partner and balance that with his need to be respected. Cheering for him is her ultimate submission to God's plan for marriage. She is to be his greatest supporter. She needs to encourage him and make sure he knows his wife is behind him no matter what.

*Robert and Rosemary Barnes*

*T*he law of love can never be a cherishing of self at the expense of the loved one, but must always be the cherishing of the loved one at the expense of self.

Hannah Whitall Smith

*E*very day we change as individuals based on our experiences that day. In order to build a growing relationship as a couple, then, we must make time to "daily reintroduce" ourselves to each other. We share the mundane and the profound. We disclose what's going on in our own lives and genuinely inquire about each other's life.

Frankly, this was fairly easy to do when we were first married and had few distractions. We had lots of time for meaningful dialogue, cups of coffee, and sharing activities together.

Now our daily reintroduction habit usually takes the form of a long walk, an extended cup of coffee (decaf, now), or a long phone call if I'm out of town. But we can testify that we depend on this habit to keep us growing, both as individuals and as a couple.

*Scott and Jill Bolinder*

# Treasure Each Other

Turn off interruptions (phone, computer, pager, TV)
and make each other your top priority.

Tell your mate five reasons why you love him or her.

Give your spouse a back rub or
scratch that unreachable itch.

Play your partner's favorite music without complaint.

Light a scented candle in the bathroom
and take a shower for two.

Take time to play and laugh with each other.

Renew your commitment to each other.

Become each other's best friend.

*L*ike separate strings of a lute that quiver with the same music, there is beauty in a marriage that respects the individuality of its partners.

*Les and Leslie Parrott*

*God created man in his own image, in the image*
*of God he created him … He created*
*them male and female and blessed them.*
Genesis 1:27, 5:2

*We have different gifts, according to the grace given us.*
Romans 12:6

*In the Lord, … woman is not independent of man, nor is man*
*independent of woman. For as woman came from man, so also*
*man is born of woman. But everything comes from God.*
1 Corinthians 11:11–12

*There are different kinds of gifts, but the same Spirit.*
*There are different kinds of service, but the same Lord.*
*There are different kinds of working, but the*
*same God works all of them in all men.*
1 Corinthians 12:4–6

*Accept one another, then, just as Christ*
*accepted you, in order to bring praise to God.*
Romans 15:7

*D*o you ever wonder if you're on the same trip as your mate? Opposites do attract; however, the very characteristic that attracted you to your mate—his or her easygoing nature, never in a hurry, always has time for people—may later be an irritation to you.

We are very different from each other, and sometimes those differences create tension in our relationship. If you will allow each other to operate in your areas of strengths and not be threatened by the other, you have the potential for building a great marriage partnership.

*David and Claudia Arp*

*I*n one sense, we have so much in common it is remarkable we don't understand each other better. We are of the same flesh. We are of the same species. We are genetically and biologically connected. Every woman receives half her DNA from a man. Every man receives half his DNA from a woman.

Yet, in another sense, men and women are as different as night from day— as beauty from the beast, as sandpaper from silk, as rose from thorn. In fact, husbands and wives are virtual opposites in almost every significant area of comparison—exactly the way God intended. Rather than a disadvantage, this diversity works the miracle of God in the sacred institution of family.

*Patrick M. Morley*

# Treasure Your Differences

Stay open to feedback and don't become defensive.

Value the things your spouse values.

Give each other the freedom to be different.

Own your own feelings, problems, choices, and attitudes.

Recognize your own need for growth and change.

View your spouse as God's gift to you.

Compromise cheerfully when necessary.

Let your spouse operate in his or her areas of
strength and learn from him or her.

Thank God for your
differences—and mean it!

*W*hat do a couple do when they differ? It all depends on how separate they are … how okay it is to have two opinions, moods, tastes, or needs in the relationship at once. What happens depends on whether a couple can tolerate differences in each other.

In a good marriage, spouses value each other's differences and treat them with respect. They understand each other, listen, reason, compromise, and give up their own wishes sometimes.

In a marriage in which the individuals aren't allowed to be different, things don't go as well. Husbands and wives judge each other as "bad" for the preferences each one has. Or they take the difference as a personal affront or a lack of love.

It is important to remember: Differences are not bad. They are part of the stuff out of which love grows.

*Dr. Henry Cloud and
Dr. John Townsend*

*H*ow do you and your partner handle differences? If you are like most couples you either sweep your differences under the rug by ignoring them altogether, or you try to make your partner become like yourself. Unfortunately, both strategies are doomed to frustration. We miss out on a tremendous gift of marriage when we do not enjoy our partner's uniqueness. That's right, enjoy the differences!

Every person is unique. God never intended couples to approach life as if they were twins separated at birth. He made us with unique strengths and weaknesses. He gave each of us special gifts. Sure, some of his or her traits make living together tough at times, but appreciating the positive side of your differences will make your marriage more balanced and complete.

*Les and Leslie Parrott*

A companionship marriage is one in which both spouses are encouraged to maximize their strengths for the benefit of the couple.

*David and Claudia Arp*

Togetherness does not imply that we will go through life hand in hand, always enjoying identical things to the same degree. We are still individual humans with divergent needs and tastes. We must respect the needs of others and compromise cheerfully when necessary.

*Cecil G. Osborne*

*B*eing different should not be a problem in marriage. In fact, it should be a benefit. When your mate has an alternative viewpoint to yours in parenting or home furnishings, you have been enriched. Your world has been enlarged. You are no longer bound to a world of your own making, which is a prison God never intended for us. You are forced to listen to, interact with, and consider the feelings and opinions of another human being in some matter in which you are dead sure you are right. If this is not a solution for human arrogance, what is!

Dr. Henry Cloud and
Dr. John Townsend

Solve Conflicts
With Love

*L*ove is not blind—it sees more, not less. But because it sees more, it is willing to see less.

*Julius Gordon*

*C*onflict is inevitable. What matters is how it is handled. Is it handled constructively, or destructively? All emotions—anger, hurt, fear—should be expressed, but considerately.

Newlyweds have a natural instinct to walk on eggshells around each other. They seem to fear being open, thinking that is the path to conflict. What they have not discovered is that the more open and honest a couple is, the greater becomes their opportunity for deeper intimacy.

### Michael J. McManus

*C*onflicts are not to be avoided. They are the warning lights. They tell us there's something that needs to be done. It doesn't mean that conflict should pit one spouse against the other. It's just the opposite. It means that the two spouses should sit down and work together to deal with the conflict.

### Robert and Rosemary Barnes

*Do not be quickly provoked in your spirit,*
*for anger resides in the lap of fools.*
Ecclesiastes 7:9

*Be kind and compassionate to one another, forgiving each other,*
*just as in Christ God forgave you.*
Ephesians 4:32

*Everyone should be quick to listen, slow to speak*
*and slow to become angry, for man's anger does not*
*bring about the righteous life that God desires.*
James 1:19–20

*Let us . . . make every effort to do what*
*leads to peace and to mutual edification.*
Romans 14:19

My most important lesson of conflict resolution in twenty-seven years of marriage is one I learned after a decade of marriage—the wisdom of Scripture that provided basic guidance on how I should deal with my conflicts with Harriet: "Do not let the sun go down while you are still angry" (Ephesians 4:26).

In other words, God expects us to be angry from time to time, but we are admonished not to allow the anger to last a long time. The relationship is always more important than any issue that divides a couple.

*Michael J. McManus*

# Fighting Fair

Be Fair—Don't hit below the belt.

Stick to the subject—Fight about one thing at a time.

Don't repeat past history—If it is more
than two days old, forget it.

No name-calling—That is character assassination.

Finish the fight—Don't walk away.

Own your involvement—Identify your own
hurtful ways and repent of them.

Resolve to change—Words and actions are needed here.

Don't go to bed mad—Ephesians 4:26: "Do not
let the sun go down while you are still angry."

*P*erhaps the greatest step toward maturity is learning how to admit when we are wrong. When we can humbly seek another's forgiveness, we not only clear the offense but also gain the respect of the offended one. What takes more courage—ignoring your offense or admitting it? The only time I ever sensed a negative reaction when I asked for forgiveness was when I asked with an accusing attitude. Not only is God drawn to the humble—so are others (James 4:6).

*Gary Smalley*

*U*se anger and conflict in a creative way to build your relationship. … A healthy marriage is a safe place to resolve honest conflict and process anger. The reason this challenge is so critical to long-term marriages is that in most conflict situations, it isn't the facts that are the real problem, it's the strong negative (or even angry) feelings we harbor. Once those feelings are dealt with, it's simple to move on and work at resolving the conflict.

*David and Claudia Arp*

*Bear with each other and forgive whatever grievances you may have against one another. Forgive as the Lord forgave you.*
Colossians 3:13

*When you stand praying, if you hold anything against anyone, forgive him, so that your Father in heaven may forgive you your sins.*
Mark 11:25

*Blessed are they whose transgressions are forgiven, whose sins are covered.*
Romans 4:7

*If anyone has caused grief, … you ought to forgive and comfort him, so that he will not be overwhelmed by excessive sorrow. I urge you, therefore, to reaffirm your love for him.*
2 Corinthians 2:5, 7–8

*Peter came to Jesus and asked, "Lord, how many times shall I forgive my brother when he sins against me? Up to seven times?" Jesus answered, "I tell you, not seven times, but seventy-seven times."*
Matthew 18:21–22

Communicate Openly
and Honestly

*C*ommunication is not just talking. It involves the willingness and capacity to express our feelings to each other.

*Cecil G. Osborne*

*T*he primary reason for communicating is not to share facts. Fact-sharing is simply the most basic form of communication. Communication at its best is defined as time spent opening the doors to one another's innermost self. Let me emphasize that by restating it: Communication is a long-term process by which two people talk in such a way as to open themselves up to one another and share who they really are.

*Robert and Rosemary Barnes*

*Y*ou have the power to bless your marriage by the words you speak to your partner. You can also bless by learning when to be silent.

*Dr. Ed Wheat*

*I*t took me years to understand a conversational difference between Harriet and me. She would describe a conflict she had with another child's mother or with a boss, and I'd listen intently. Then I'd suggest a solution: Tell her this, or tell him that. She'd blow up: "My purpose in telling you was to share my frustration and to have a listening ear. If I don't talk to you, whom am I going to talk to?" I was just trying to suggest how to solve the problem—a role any male would understand. She didn't want to solve it, only describe it! Our miscommunication is typical. Much verbal conflict is rooted in simple male-female differences.

*Michael J. McManus*

An ad in a Kansas newspaper said, "I will listen to you talk without comment for thirty minutes for five dollars." Would you believe that ten to twenty people called every day from all over the United States just to have someone listen to them?

This reaffirms how very important it is to have someone listen; in marriage, that someone needs to be your mate.

In James 1:19 we are told, "Everyone should be quick to listen, slow to speak and slow to become angry."

In our actions, we too often rephrase this verse to, "Be slow to listen and very quick to speak and become angry." If we can slow our words and reactions, perhaps we could be better listeners. But don't just listen for words—listen for the feelings as well.

*David and Claudia Arp*

When wives befriend, encourage, help, respect, and support their husbands they take a huge step toward inoculating their marriages against death by broken heart.

It is true that more men are developing strong male friendships through accountability groups, but even there remains certain guardedness. As Oswald Chambers said, "What is the sign of a friend? That he tells you secret sorrows? No, that he tells you secret joys. Many will confide to you their secret sorrows, but the last mark of intimacy is to confide secret joys."

*Patrick M. Morley*

*I*ntimacy has a "best friend" or "soul mate" quality about it. We all want someone who knows us better than anyone else—and still accepts us. And we want someone who holds nothing back from us, someone who trusts us with personal secrets. Intimacy fills our heart's deepest longings for closeness and acceptance.

*Les and Leslie Parrott*

*T*here are two kinds of people in the world: those who focus on what they want, always desiring it and never attaining it, and those who focus on what it takes to obtain what they want. The latter do the work, delay gratification, make sacrifices, and ultimately get the rewards of their work.

In marriage, if you focus on what you want and desire and just stay angry and disappointed that you are not getting it, you will remain there. But if you focus on cultivating the garden instead of demanding the fruit, then your garden will yield a huge harvest. Give time, money, energy, focus, and other resources to developing the love of God and each other, honesty, faithfulness, compassion, forgiveness, and holiness. Pursue them with everything the two of you can muster. They will not fail you in the end.

Dr. Henry Cloud and
Dr. John Townsend

*I*t is by meaningful conversation that we scale the heights and plumb the depths of marriage.

Discussing facts enables you to connect at the head level. Discussing feelings enables you to connect at the heart level. Connecting at the level of the head will get the task done, but only by connecting our hearts to each other can we become the intimate soul mates of our dreams. Keep the focus on connecting your hearts rather than winning the battle of the minds.

*Patrick M. Morley*

# Share With Each Other

Take turns listening to one another intently without thinking of what you are going to say next.

Pay close attention to nonverbal communication—tone of voice, body language, and facial expressions. Many times they say more than the words ever could.

Express your positive feelings, not just the negative ones.

Let your spouse know when they do or say something that you appreciate.

Schedule a few minutes of quiet time each day to reconnect and catch up with each other.

Trust Each Other

*I*t is a greater compliment
to be trusted than to be loved.

*George MacDonald*

$O$ne of the words the Bible uses for trust means to be so confident that you can be "care-less." In other words, you don't have to worry. You are so "taken care of" that you don't have to take care yourself. You can trust that what was promised will be done.

It means that your spouse can be certain that you will deliver on what you have promised. It could mean being sexually faithful, but it could also mean doing chores faithfully! It could mean staying within the monthly budget and coming home when you say you will. It could mean sharing without fear of reprisal or condemnation. You can rest in the knowledge that what needs to get done will get done. This is a beautiful picture of faithfulness.

Dr. Henry
Cloud and
Dr. John
Townsend

*L*ove is the greatest gift and the greatest risk. To be completely open with the one whose opinion matters most, requires deep trust. It's a difficult balance to achieve in marriage, this standing on the precipice of understanding and rejection. That the risk is worth the result in no way makes it easier to be transparent with one another. God knows how we feel, though. He risked his own Son to reach out and let a world of fallen people into his heart. He'll help you learn to trust one another as you learn to trust him.

*Pat Matuszak*

*T*he expression of confidence in your mate is important. Your wife's heart should be able to trust in you as the one who will always be there when needed, helping and not hurting, because you are her husband and because her happiness and security mean as much to you as your own.

A wife can help her husband by listening, understanding, and sympathizing with his problems; then by communicating her confidence in his ability to solve the problems and remove the obstacles. He does not need mothering or a dose of positive thinking or even advice, sensible though that may be. Instead, he needs reassurance from his wife that she has confidence in him, that she sees him as a man capable of conquering his environment. Each partner should be to the other a haven of refuge from the harshness of the outside world.

*Dr. Ed Wheat*

*I* believe that every self-confident type like myself needs ... to walk in the front door, look at the wife who loves him, swallow a couple of times and then say, "Well, uh, guess what—come Monday morning, I won't be going anywhere." The pain of that confession cuts you down to size, confronts you with your inadequacies, humbles you, makes you vulnerable. And in your helplessness, the two of you are drawn closer together.

You find yourselves leaning on each other, praying desperately for divine help, and at the same time counting the blessings that remain. In our case, we had to wait five weeks before I went to work again, whereas others have hung in limbo much longer. But in the long run, it was the steady confidence of my wife and the knowledge that God was still in control that held the pieces together.

*Dean Merrill*

*A wife of noble character who can find? She is worth far more than rubies. Her husband has full confidence in her and lacks nothing of value. She brings him good, not harm, all the days of her life.*
Proverbs 31:10–12

*In God our hearts rejoice, for we trust in his holy name. May your unfailing love rest upon us, O LORD, even as we put our hope in you.*
Psalm 33:21–22

*It is required that those who have been given a trust must prove faithful.*
1 Corinthians 4:2

*Those who know your name will trust in you, for you, LORD, have never forsaken those who seek you.*
Psalm 9:10

*O*ur commitment to each other in marriage is sustained by God's model of faithfulness to us. Without commitment and the trust it engenders, marriage would have no hope of enduring.

*Les and Leslie Parrott*

*A* commitment to growth goes beyond just sticking together. It's also a commitment to adapt to each other's changing needs. Adapting to each other requires self-sacrifice. It calls for thinking of the other person and looking for ways to grow with and adapt to each other's changing needs. It means being that one person the other can always count on.

*David and Claudia Arp*

Respect And Honor
Each Other

$L$ove has nothing to do with
what you are expecting to get,
it's what you are expecting to
give—which is everything.

Anonymous

" *The* more we value something, the more gentle we will be in handling it." If I handed you a three-thousand-year-old, paper thin Oriental vase worth $50,000 and asked you to take it to the bank, would you handle it differently than if I gave you a fifty-nine-cent plastic vase and asked you to take it down the street?

*Gary Smalley*

*i*t seems to me that little things I do for Patsy make deposits into her emotional bank account that far exceed their value. The little things often carry more weight than some of the big things. Why? My wife expects me to handle the big things right. When I do the little things right she is pleasantly surprised.

Many people don't think the little things are all that important. They are wrong. Dead wrong. "It's the little things that count." Small kindnesses. A loving glance. A chore done in secret that is discovered. Consistency. Dependability. Honesty.

Remember. Anyone can do the big things right ... but it's the little things that count. Handle the little things well and you will be given much.

*Patrick M. Morley*

# Commandments for a Happy Marriage

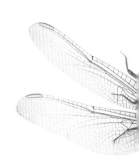

Always try to put your best foot forward.
(Dress, speech, and manners that are as
desirable after marriage as before.)

Make it a priority to show
appreciation to your mate every day.

Reserve time for one another.

Strive always to be patient when your
partner has had a rough day.
(Tension time is a time for patience.)

Be willing to admit your faults and say, "I'm sorry."

Remember that love is a two-way street. (The most
intimate relationship should be a mutual adventure.)

Stand together in the great events of life. (Not "his home," but "our home." Not "my baby," but "our baby.")

Be careful not to throw a spark into spilled gasoline. (Some marital problems are like spilled gasoline, ready to ignite when the wrong word is spoken.)

Find joy in serving God together. (Not even church activities should be permitted to keep husbands and wives apart several nights each week.)

Receive strength by meeting God together at the end of each day. (Prayer before retiring makes married life inspiring.)

*H*eidi and I realized early in our marriage that a prerequisite to intimacy of any kind was a foundation of respect for each other and for our relationship. As a result we've tried to keep out destructive attitudes. This entails:

Not discussing problems in harsh, angry tones, but in attentive conversation.

Not joking cuttingly about each other, especially in front of others.

Never kidding about divorce.

Saving constructive criticism for when we're alone and in a receptive frame of mind.

Being willing to give in to each other's preferences—saying, "this is really important to me."

Regularly giving verbal and nonverbal encouragement to make the other person feel treasured.

*Mark and Heidi Mittelberg*

*W*e all have our own ideas about what love means. To some it is romance, and to others it is security. To still others, it is the feeling of being attracted to some quality that another possesses, such as power and achievement.

[But] the love that builds a marriage is the kind of love God has for us. It is called "agape." Agape is love that seeks the welfare of the other. It is love that has nothing to do with how someone is gratifying us at the moment. It has to do with what is good for *the other*.

Jesus said it this way in the second greatest commandment: "Love your neighbor as yourself" (Matthew 22:39). When we do that, we are truly loving someone.

Dr. Henry Cloud and
Dr. John Townsend

*Marriage should be honored by all.*
Hebrews 13:4

*My lover is radiant and ruddy,*
*outstanding among ten thousand.*
Song of Songs 5:10

*Honor one another above yourselves.*
Romans 12:10

*My dove in the clefts of the rock,*
*in the hiding places on the mountainside,*
*show me your face,*
*let me hear your voice;*
*for your voice is sweet,*
*and your face is lovely.*
Song of Songs 2:14

The Christian husband is the guy who resists the temptation to use a wife joke to get a laugh. If he has a bone to pick with his wife, he does it straight-forwardly and in private.

The evidence of love is often contained in words. Public words, private words. Words *to* our wives, words *about* our wives. Words—the right kind of honest and affirming words—are the stepping stones with which we build the castle of marriage.

Most of us have the common courtesy not to make negative remarks about our boss or a colleague at work. Why should you sound off about your in-laws? No matter how perceptive your comments, they will raise your wife's defenses and serve no useful purpose.

Dean Merrill

As human beings, we all need and respond to praise. There is nothing shameful about longing for an occasional "pat on the back."

*Gary Smalley*

When we do have positive, tender thoughts, often we keep them to ourselves. Positive thoughts are worth expressing! Begin by making your own list of what you appreciate about your spouse. Dwell on your mate's positive qualities. Keep on turning those positive thoughts into verbal affirmation. Think of it as a positive verbal recycle bin. Develop the habit of praising each other. We can have all kinds of nice thoughts about our mates, but power is only released when they are verbalized.

*David and Claudia Arp*

# Respect Each Other

Never again be critical of your partner in word, thought, or deed.

Become sensitive to the areas where your partner feels a lack.
Build up your partner in those areas.

Verbalize praise and appreciation. Be genuine, specific, generous.

Communicate your respect for the work he or she does.

Husband, show your wife publicly and privately how precious
she is to you. Do not express admiration for another woman.
Keep your attention focused on your wife!

Wife, show your husband that he is the most important person
in your life—always. Seek his opinions; value his judgment.

Respond to each other facially. Your mate wants to see
you smile, eyes sparkling in response to him or her.

Exhibit the greatest courtesy to each other. You should be
VIPs in your own home!

*Dr. Ed Wheat*

Be Best Friends

*L*et the wife make her husband glad
to come home and let him make her
sorry to see him leave.

*Martin Luther*

$\mathcal{D}$o you consider your spouse your best friend? Do you look for ways to spend time together? Do you laugh together? Do you have fun with each other? All are symptoms of friendship and symptoms of a great marriage.

Maybe you've been neglecting your friendship. The cares and concerns of providing for your family can be so overwhelming that you overlook having fun together. But in a healthy marriage and love life, having fun is serious business.

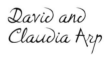

*David and Claudia Arp*

*B*eing a friend requires decisive action. It necessitates asking oneself questions like, "How can I help this person that I love?" Of course, this applies not just to the big things in life, but also to the little day-to-day things such as dishes, or whatever those little special gestures happen to be.

So often many of us feel that we plug away through life doing the hard things, making a living, painting the house, ironing the clothes, things that are the long-haul gestures. If we do those things, many of us believe we're doing enough. But those are obligatory. Rather than gestures, they are responsibilities. Friends do things that go beyond obligation.

*Robert and Rosemary Barnes*

# Treasure Each Other
## as Friends

Develop a shared interest, activity or sport.

Share secrets.

Take turns initiating love-making.

Look for ways to compromise.

Enjoy each other's company.

Encourage each other with words.

Keep the lines of communication open—talk about
everything; keep short accounts.

Learn something new together;
a course; a tour; a new kind of food or music.

Laugh together.

Make each other your top priority.

*H*aving a healthy, growing marriage relationship requires friendship, fun, and romance. And there's no better way to encourage all of these things than having dates! Great dates are more than going to see a movie and tuning out the world for a while. Great dates involve communicating with one another, reviving the spark that initially ignited your fire, and developing mutual interests and goals that are not focused on your careers or your children. Great dates can revitalize your relationship. Here are five great dating ideas:

*Formal-dinner-in-the-park date:* Put on your black tie and evening gown and grab a picnic basket for an evening under the stars!

*I'm-just-too-tired date:* Order takeout, turn on the answering machine, and just relax and enjoy snuggling while you read or watch a movie.

*Photo date:* Go to your favorite haunt and snap away. Simply set the timer on your camera and run back and smile!

*Gourmet-cooking date:* If you ever wanted to take up gourmet cooking, do it together and call it a date! Plan the menu, grocery shop together at an upscale market, and cook your dinner together!

*Proposal date:* Go to a public place and ask your mate to marry you all over again!

*David and Claudia Arp*

*Two are better than one, because they have a good return for*
*their work: If one falls down, his friend can help him up.*
*But pity the man who falls and has no one to help him up!*
*Also, if two lie down together, they will keep warm.*
*But how can one keep warm alone?*
Ecclesiastes 4:9–11

*The pleasantness of one's friend*
*springs from his earnest counsel.*
Proverbs 27:9

*His mouth is sweetness itself; he is altogether lovely.*
*This is my lover, this my friend.*
Song of Songs 5:16

*A friend loves at*
*all times.*
Proverbs 17:17

*Jesus said, "Greater love has no one than this,*
*that he lay down his life for his friends."*
John 15:13

*N*o marriage is invulnerable. I had many interests, ambitions, and priorities. Patsy was not my top priority. In many ways I viewed her as another human resource to help me achieve my dreams. The Holy Spirit showed me the truth. I was using Patsy. Before the Lord I repented, and he showed me how to make Patsy my best friend.

Without announcing my intentions, I started hanging around the dinner table after the kids left. For twenty minutes I would ask her about her day, her dreams, her hopes, her fears. I wanted to get to know this woman who had knocked me off my feet over a dozen years earlier. Within a few weeks we were on the road to becoming best friends. Not long after Patsy gave me a plaque for my desk. It read, "Happiness is being married to your best friend." Thank you, Jesus.

*Patrick M. Morley*

Build Simple
Memories

*H*ow vast a memory has Love!

*Alexander Pope*

*D*own through the centuries men and women have employed various means of expressing their love to one another. I suppose if you're gifted at writing songs, you have, like many others, written a song to the one you love. If you're able to go one step beyond and put your lyrics to music, all the better! But then, if you are *particularly* gifted, or courageous, and dare to *sing* this song to your beloved, that's the best! There is something very special about singing your own words of love to your sweetheart.

*Charles R. Swindoll*

*W*hat attracted you to your mate when you first met? What do you think attracted your mate to you? What about your first date? Do you remember the first time you talked about getting married? What do you remember about your wedding day?

It's fun to think back into our history and remember the excitement of that time when we realized we were in love. Memories help us to remember just how important our marriage is and why we want to keep nurturing our relationship. They motivate us today to make our marriage a high priority. Revisiting your memories will help affirm that your marriage is also a high priority!

*David and Claudia Arp*

*Let him kiss me with the kisses of his mouth—*
*for your love is more delightful than wine.*
Song of Songs 1:2

*My lover spoke and said to me,*
*"Arise, my darling, my beautiful one, and come with me.*
*See! The winter is past; the rains are over and gone. Flowers*
*appear on the earth; the season of singing has come,*
*the cooing of doves is heard in our land. The fig tree forms*
*its early fruit; the blossoming vines spread their fragrance.*
*Arise, come, my darling; my beautiful one, come with me."*
Song of Songs 2:10–13

*I belong to my lover, and his desire is for me. Come, my lover,*
*let us go to the countryside, let us spend the night in the villages.*
*Let us go early to the vineyards to see if the vines have budded,*
*if their blossoms have opened, and if the pomegranates are*
*in bloom—there I will give you my love.*
Song of Songs 7:10–12

We can give leisure its proper place in our lives. Vacations are probably more strategic for our wives than for ourselves. Why? Because wives carry the major responsibility for the work of the household seven days a week. In terms of pure recycling and change of scenery, she is the neediest.

As a matter of fact, vacations are but part of the relief she needs. Weekend dinners and excursions are even more refreshing for her than for us. They don't have to be expensive.

You might want to sit down with your wife sometime and make a list of all the things the two of you could do for less than five dollars. Keep adding to the list as things come to your mind and as friends happen to mention places they've gone and evenings they've enjoyed.

Dean Merrill

# Memories to Treasure

Leave a romantic message on your spouse's e-mail or
answering machine at work.

Place a flower or love note under the
windshield wiper of his or her car.

Pick up your mate's favorite candy bar
the next time you're shopping.

Send a card to your spouse to say thanks for
being your friend, soul mate, lover.

Give your partner a foot massage.

Learn to line dance or square dance.

Play a sport together.

Buy a season ticket to the theater or symphony.

Take a cooking class together.

Learn a hobby together.

*F*rom our Marriage Alive seminar participants we gathered information on what couples who are best friends are doing for fun. Here are some of their responses:

We like to take the back roads, get lost, and then find our way home again.

We like to cook together. Lately, we've been learning to cook Chinese.

We pick berries together.

We learned to sail together.

We like to rock in our double rocker on our screened porch.

One night we slept out on our balcony under the stars.

We like to read aloud together.

*David and Claudia Arp*

*D*ecide to be spontaneous. When one spouse suggests doing something, the other spouse needs to choose to get the energy to do it.

Pull out the nails that are holding you down to your routine or couch. Pull out the nails that have you stuck to the television. Don't wait for friends to invite you to do things that are fun. Choose to do fun things as a husband and wife. You'll be amazed how much energy you really have. You'll also be surprised how much it will mean to your marriage.

*Robert and Rosemary Barnes*

**W**e decided early in our marriage to establish a regularly scheduled "date night"! Just the two of us, alone. To laugh, to lift our spirits, to love. It puts the two of us more at ease with each other during the remainder of the week.

It's hard to imagine what our marriage would be like today if we had not had our weekly date night. Because we are changing persons in a changing world, we are constantly becoming reacquainted with each other. As a result, we have grown together—not apart—as the years have passed. How blessed are those who experience the priceless discovery of love!

*Robert and
Arvella Schuller*

Worship God
Together

*B*ut nought can break the union
Of hearts in Thee made one;
And love Thy Spirit hallows
Is endless love begun.

*John Ellerton*

*I rejoiced with those who said to me,*
*"Let us go to the house of the LORD."*
Psalm 122:1

*You are a chosen people, a royal priesthood, a holy nation, a*
*people belonging to God, that you may declare the praises of him*
*who called you out of darkness into his wonderful light.*
1 Peter 2:9

*Jesus said, "I tell you that if two of you on earth agree*
*about anything you ask for, it will be done for you*
*by my Father in heaven. For where two or three*
*come together in my name, there am I with them."*
Matthew 18:19–20

*I will sing to the LORD,*
*for he has been good to me.*
Psalm 13:6

Our path to spiritual understanding was illuminated by God's love, acceptance, and forgiveness, which, to this day, touch us to our very core. As God began to be more real to us in our own personal lives, we began to experience spiritual intimacy in our marriage. It was as if we had been plugged into a new power source. Finding our security and significance in our Creator freed us to love and accept each other in a deeper way.

As we developed intimacy with God, we began to pray together. Having spiritual intimacy helped us open up to each other—and share our most private hopes and fears in all areas of our lives. Our faith directly influences our love life, giving it a spiritual dimension.

*David and Claudia Arp*

*W*hat about spiritual growth and your marriage? If your spouse is a partner who believes as you do, a worthy goal would be to decide to pray together each night. If your spouse does not believe as you do, then decide to find a time to pray for him or her each night.

Rare is the couple who are at the same place of spiritual growth all the time. Most couples vary when it comes to which is the person who is the most spiritually "tuned in" at any particular time.

*Robert and Rosemary Barnes*

*P*aul says to "spur one another on toward love and good deeds" (Hebrews 10:24). Marriage helps us do just that, and when we join our efforts in service together we are doubly blessed.

There are literally hundreds of ways to incorporate shared service into your marriage—offering hospitality in your home, volunteering at a shelter, sponsoring a needy child, working in the church nursery. The key is to find something that fits your personal style.

As a partnership, two people can serve other people better than they could as separate individuals. So don't neglect the practice of shared service. It will do more to enrich the soul of your marriage than you can ever imagine.

*Les and Leslie Parrott*

*W*e have a Norman Rockwell print that depicts a family on Sunday morning. The husband, unshaven, messy-haired, and ensconced in pajamas and bathrobe, is slumped in a chair with portions of the Sunday paper strewn about. Behind him is his wife dressed in a tailored suit and on her way to church. The picture is a playful reminder to us of how important shared worship is to the soul of our marriage.

When we got married and moved far from home, worship was suddenly an option. For the first time, going to church was something we were not compelled to do. … Nobody was checking up on us. We could now stay home on Sundays, take a hike, sit in the sun, read a book. Or we could go to church. We did.

The church where we worship is a place of social support and spiritual refueling. Singing hymns, learning from Scripture, worshiping God, and meeting with friends who share our spiritual quest is comforting and inspiring. Worshiping together buoys our relationship and makes the week ahead more meaningful.

*Les and Leslie
Parrott*

*N*othing our spouse can do for us can touch us so deeply as faithfully praying for us day after day—long after the normal person would have moved on to something new. Praying for our mate is another way of saying "I love you." It is an expression of loyalty to our partner. We say by our prayers that we are committed to bless and be a blessing to our mate. Our prayers help unlock the rich treasures of God's kingdom for our spouse.

When we pray for each other we deepen our partner's love for us. Through a spiritual operation our loving and gracious Father sews our hearts more closely together. Our heart is bonded to our partner when we know he/she is bringing petitions for us before the throne of God's grace.

*Patrick M. Morley*

*G*race and I have had some exciting periods of studying the Bible and praying together. A couple of times each year it seems like one says to the other, "Hey, let's have devotions together for a while."

When we have moved on to pray together, the synergism has been even more beneficial. We just sort of let it all come out before the Lord. Grace prays, I pray, we wait and listen. Sometimes we go whole paragraphs, sometimes just a sentence or two, the same way a normal conversation runs. No speechmaking is allowed, or even desired.

Sometimes we kneel, sometimes we sit, and sometimes we keep our eyes open. Inevitably, we come away sensing that our heads have been cleared. (And we usually end up kicking ourselves for not making time to do this more often.)

*Dean Merrill*

# Habits for a Successful Love Life

Married couples who have a successful love life:

Make time to dream and plan together.

Develop the habit of dating.

Give each other the freedom to grow and change.

Practice the habits of forgiveness and acceptance.

Concentrate on the positive and build each other up.

Possess a sense of humor.

Know how to be best friends and have fun together.

Continue to learn how to be better mates.

Make time for intimacy.

Make their marriage a priority.

David and Claudia Arp

Arp, David and Claudia. *Love Life for Parents.* Grand Rapids, MI: ZondervanPublishingHouse, 1998. *Ten Great Dates to Revitalize Your Marriage.* Grand Rapids, MI: ZondervanPublishingHouse, 1997.

Barnes, Robert and Rosemary. *Rock-Solid Marriage.* Grand Rapids, MI: ZondervanPublishingHouse, 1993.

Cloud, Dr. Henry, and Dr. John Townsend. *Boundaries in Marriage.* Grand Rapids, MI: ZondervanPublishingHouse, 1999.

Crabb, Dr. Larry. *The Marriage Builder.* Grand Rapids, MI: Zondervan Corporation, 1976.

Hefley, James C. *A Dictionary of Illustrations.* Grand Rapids, MI: ZondervanPublishingHouse, 1976.

McManus, Michael J. *Marriage Savers.* Grand Rapids, MI: ZondervanPublishingHouse, 1995.

Merrill, Dean. *How to Really Love Your Wife.* Grand Rapids, MI: Zondervan Corporation, 1977.

Morley, Patrick M. *Devotions for Couples.* Grand Rapids, MI: ZondervanPublishingHouse, 1994.

Osborne, Cecil G. *How to Have a Happier Wife.* Grand Rapids, MI: Zondervan Corporation, 1970.

Parrott, Les and Leslie. *Becoming Soul Mates.* Grand Rapids, MI: ZondervanPublishingHouse, 1995.

Richards, Dr. Lawrence O. *The Parenting Bible.* Grand Rapids, MI: Zondervan Corporation, 1994.

Smalley, Gary. *How to Become Your Husband's Best Friend.* Grand Rapids, MI: Zondervan Corporation, 1982.

Sweeting, George. *Who Said That?* Chicago: Moody Press. 1995.

Swindoll, Charles R. *The Living Insights Study Bible.* Grand Rapids, MI: Zondervan Corporation, 1996.

Wheat, Ed, MD. *Love Life for Every Married Couple.* Grand Rapids, MI: ZondervanPublishingHouse, 1980.

White, R.E.O. *You Can Say That Again.* Grand Rapids, MI: ZondervanPublishingHouse, 1991.

loving

for life

for life

loving

loving

for life

loving

for life

loving

loving

for life